Life at Home

Sharon Coan, M.S.Ed.

They live in a big **city**.

We live in a big city.

This is their home.

This is our home.

They cook dinner.

We cook dinner.

They wash dishes.

We wash dishes.

They buy clothes.

We buy clothes.

They go many **places**.

We go many places.

They play with friends.

We play with friends.

They like their home.

We like our home.

Draw It!

1. Think about your home.
2. What do you do at home?

3. Draw a picture.

Glossary

city—a large town

places—parts of the world

Index

Your Turn!

Home is a special place. What do you like about your home? Tell a friend.

Consultants

Shelley Scudder
Gifted Teacher
Broward County Schools

Caryn Williams, M.S.Ed.
Madison County Schools
Huntsville, AL

Publishing Credits

Conni Medina, M.A.Ed., *Managing Editor*
Lee Aucoin, *Creative Director*
Torrey Maloof, *Editor*
Lexa Hoang, *Designer*
Stephanie Reid, *Photo Editor*
Rachelle Cracchiolo, M.S.Ed., *Publisher*

Image Credits: Cover, p.1 Blue Jean Images/Alamy; p.17 Golden Pixels LLC/Alamy; p.3 Wendy Connett/Alamy; p.5 Blue Jean Images/Alamy; p.7 Wavebreak Media ltd/Alamy; p.16 Bert Hardy/Getty Image; p.6 H. Armstrong Roberts/Getty Images; p.12 Hulton Archive/Getty Images; p.10 Three Lions/Getty Images; p.14 Time & Life Pictures/Getty Image; p.13 somethingway/iStockphoto; p.23 Diana Kenney; p.2 LOC [LC-D401-12683]/The Library of Congress; p.8 LOC [LC-DIG-fsa-8e10821]/The Library of Congress; p.4 LC-DIG-nclc-04667/The Library of Congress; p.22 LC-DIG-ppmsc-00046/The Library of Congress; p.19 Teacher Created Materials; All other images from Shutterstock.

Teacher Created Materials
5301 Oceanus Drive
Huntington Beach, CA 92649-1030
http://www.tcmpub.com

ISBN 978-1-4333-7338-1

Printed in Malaysia
Thumbprints.42285